Healthy
Slow Cooking
More Flavor, Fewer Calories

First published in 2010 in the United States of America by
Filipacchi Publishing
1633 Broadway
New York, NY 10019

ISBN-13: 978-1-936297-02-3

Library of Congress Control Number: 2010921564

Design: D'Mello+Felmus Design Inc.
Editor: Lauren Kuczala
Manufacturing: Lynn Scaglione

Printed in China

Healthy
Slow Cooking
More Flavor, Fewer Calories

Woman's Day

Contents

Dos &

1. Brown large cuts of meat before adding them to your cooker to ensure they reach food-safety temperature standards.

2. Gently wash your cooker's insert with hot soapy water so it's completely clean before using it. And allow the insert to cool completely after cooking before cleaning and storing it.

3. Thaw frozen foods in the refrigerator overnight before adding them to your slow cooker. Skipping this step will increase the time necessary for food to reach a safe temperature. Improperly thawed food makes slow-cooked dishes cook unevenly.

4. Place the foods that take longer to cook on the bottom of the cooker insert, then arrange the other solid ingredients on top, spreading them as evenly as possible so they cook at about the same time. Pour in liquid ingredients last.

5. Spraying the cooker insert with nonstick cooking spray before filling it will make cleanup much quicker and easier.

6. When your recipe is finished, be sure to turn off and unplug the slow cooker before you remove the finished dish. Doing so prevents the base unit from remaining heated after your recipe is complete.

7. Add the more tender ingredients, such as peas, zucchini, fish and mushrooms, during the last half-hour to one hour of cooking. This allows them to impart their flavors without becoming mushy due to overcooking.

8. Read the recipe you're using carefully—it will usually tell you at what point you should test the food for doneness. And don't forget to wear oven mitts when you do—both the lid and the cooker insert can get very hot!

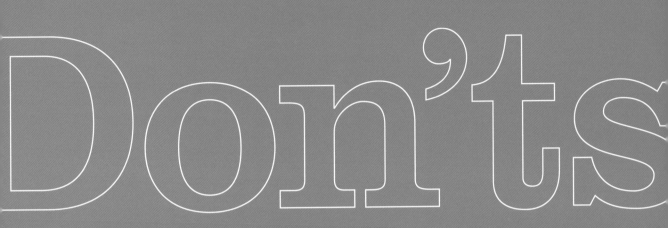

Don'ts

1. Using abrasive sponges and cleansers to clean the cooker insert will scratch and damage it.

2. Don't remove the cover of your slow cooker during cooking unless the recipe says to. Doing so will cause the loss of valuable heat.

3. Never reheat leftovers in your slow cooker. It won't reach a high enough temperature in time to meet food-safety standards. Use the microwave instead.

4. Don't put the cooker insert over direct heat, such as a gas or electric burner. Extreme or sudden temperature changes can cause breakage. For the same reason, you shouldn't use the insert in the oven or put it in the freezer.

5. Overfilling your slow cooker can be dangerous. Halfway to two-thirds full is the ideal fill quotient. It ensures optimal cooking.

6. Don't add dairy products until the last half-hour to one hour of cooking time. When cooked for too long or at too-high temperatures, dairy products tend to curdle and separate.

7. Never store leftovers in your slow cooker insert. Always transfer leftovers to separate containers or ziptop bags and either refrigerate or freeze them.

8. Slow cookers should not be placed near an open window or in the path of a draft. This interferes with their ability to reach the correct cooking temperature.

9. Preheating your slow cooker isn't necessary unless the recipe you're using specifies doing so.

10. Don't stir food in the cooker unless the recipe instructions say to. One of the many advantages of slow cooking is that it keeps foods from sticking or bubbling over, making stirring unnecessary.

Hungarian Beef Stew

Serves 6 (makes 8 cups)
Active: 10 min
Total: 8 to 10 hr on low

1¼ lb lean beef chuck for stew, cut in ¾-in. pieces
1 lb carrots, sliced
2 medium onions, thinly sliced
3 cups thinly sliced cabbage
2 cups water, or ½ cup red wine plus 1½ cups water
1 can (6 oz) tomato paste
1 envelope onion-mushroom soup mix (from a 1.8-oz box)
1 Tbsp paprika
1 tsp caraway seeds
1 cup (8 oz) reduced-fat sour cream
Serve with: egg noodles

❶ Mix all ingredients except sour cream in a 3½-qt or larger slow cooker.
❷ Cover and cook on low 8 to 10 hours until tender. Turn off cooker and stir in sour cream until well blended.

Per serving: 308 calories, 24 g protein, 25 g carbohydrates, 6 g fiber, 13 g fat (5 g saturated fat), 74 mg cholesterol, 624 mg sodium

Beef Gyros

Serves 5
Active: 10 min
Total: 6 to 8 hr on low

1 slow cooker liner
2 lb boneless beef chuck steak, about 1¼ in. thick
¼ cup olive oil
2 Tbsp lemon juice
1 Tbsp minced garlic
1 tsp dried oregano
½ tsp salt
¼ tsp pepper

Yogurt-Dill Sauce
1 cup Greek yogurt
1 cup diced seedless cucumber
1 Tbsp snipped fresh dill
¼ tsp salt

5 pocketless pita breads
Accompaniments: leaf lettuce, sliced tomatoes and red onions

❶ Line a 3-qt or larger slow cooker with liner; place beef in liner.
❷ Mix oil, lemon juice, garlic, oregano, salt and pepper in small bowl. Pour over beef, turning to coat. Cover and cook on low 6 to 8 hours until meat is tender.
❸ Meanwhile, make Sauce: Stir ingredients together, cover and refrigerate.
❹ Remove beef to cutting board; slice. Return beef to juices in slow cooker to keep warm. Warm pitas as package directs; top with sliced meat. Serve with accompaniments and yogurt sauce.

Per serving: 722 calories, 52 g protein, 33 g carbohydrates, 2 g fiber, 42 g fat (13 g saturated fat), 128 mg cholesterol, 818 mg sodium

Chinese Orange Beef

Serves 5
Active: 10 min
Total: 8 to 10 hr on low, plus 10 min on high

1 slow cooker liner
2 lb cubed beef stew meat
½ cup teriyaki sauce
½ cup orange marmalade
1 tsp each minced garlic and fresh ginger
1 red pepper, cut in ½-in.-thick strips
6 oz snow peas, strings removed
4 scallions, thinly sliced

❶ Line a 3-qt or larger slow cooker with liner. Add beef, teriyaki sauce, orange marmalade, garlic and ginger to slow cooker. Cover and cook on low 8 to 10 hours until beef is tender.
❷ Turn to high. Stir in pepper strips and snow peas; cover and cook on high 10 minutes or until vegetables are crisp-tender. Top with scallions.

Per serving: 572 calories, 38 g protein, 30 g carbohydrates, 2 g fiber, 33 g fat (13 g saturated fat), 120 mg cholesterol, 1,110 mg sodium

Stuffed Cabbage with Cranberry & Tomato Sauce

Serves 6
Active: 35 min
Total: 7½ hr on low

1½ lb lean ground beef
⅓ cup uncooked parboiled (converted) rice
1 large egg
¾ tsp ground allspice
1 tsp salt
½ tsp pepper
12 savoy cabbage leaves (see Note)
1 can (16 oz) whole-berry cranberry sauce
1 can (14.5 oz) diced tomatoes with onion and garlic
½ cup raisins, preferably golden
⅓ cup packed light-brown sugar
¼ cup fresh lemon juice

❶ You'll need a 5-qt or larger slow cooker.
❷ Mix first 6 ingredients in a bowl. Spoon a slightly rounded ¼ cup of mixture on bottom center of each cabbage leaf; turn in sides and roll up.
❸ Stack in cooker, seam sides down. Top with remaining ingredients. Cover and cook on low 7 hours or until cabbage is soft and meat mixture is cooked through.

Note: The crinkled leaves of savoy cabbage are quite soft and pliable, so precooking is unnecessary. Cut the hard rib from each leaf. If savoy cabbage is unavailable, freeze a head of regular green cabbage at least 24 hours. As the head thaws, the leaves should become soft and peel off easily.

Per serving: 584 calories, 24 g protein, 67 g carbohydrates, 2 g fiber, 24 g fat (10 g saturated fat), 121 mg cholesterol, 821 mg sodium

Boardwalk Italian Beef

Serves 6
Active: 10 min
Total: 8 to 10 hr on low

3-lb beef rump roast, trimmed of visible fat
1 medium onion, thinly sliced
½ cup water
1 jar (11 or 12 oz) pepperoncini peppers, sliced (reserve ½ cup juice)
1 pouch (0.7 oz) Italian salad dressing mix (we used Good Seasons)
2 tsp minced garlic
6 hoagie or hero rolls, split
Serve with: arugula, tomato slices

❶ Place beef and onion in a 3½-qt or larger slow cooker. Add water, pepper juice, salad dressing mix and garlic. (If you have time, cover and place in the refrigerator to let beef marinate for several hours, turning occasionally.)
❷ Cover and cook on low 8 to 10 hours until beef is very tender.
❸ Brush cut sides of rolls with some of the cooking liquid.
❹ Transfer beef to cutting board; slice thinly. Serve on rolls with arugula, sliced tomatoes and sliced peppers.

Per serving: 650 calories, 51 g protein, 76 g carbohydrates, 4 g fiber, 15 g fat (4 g saturated fat), 91 mg cholesterol, 1,600 mg sodium

Pot Roast with Vegetables

Serves 6
Active: 12 min
Total: 8 to 10 hr on low

1 can (10.75 oz) condensed cream of mushroom soup with roasted garlic
1 box (2.2 oz) beefy onion soup mix (2 pkts)
⅓ cup dry red wine
1 tsp dried rosemary, crushed
2 cloves garlic, thinly sliced
3-lb boneless beef chuck roast
4 carrots, cut in 2-in. lengths; thick pieces halved lengthwise
2 parsnips, peeled, cut in 2-in. lengths; thick pieces halved lengthwise
5 medium red-skinned potatoes, sliced ½ in. thick
Garnish: chopped fresh dill

❶ Whisk soup, soup mix, wine, rosemary and garlic in an oval 5½-qt or larger slow cooker until blended. Add beef; turn to coat. Arrange carrots, parsnips and potatoes around meat.
❷ Cover and cook on low 8 to 10 hours, until meat and vegetables are tender.
❸ Remove meat to cutting board and slice. Place on serving platter. Remove vegetables with a slotted spoon; arrange around beef. Spoon some gravy on meat; sprinkle with dill. Serve remaining gravy at the table.

Per serving: 714 calories, 43 g protein, 45 g carbohydrates, 6 g fiber, 39 g fat (15 g saturated fat), 151 mg cholesterol, 1,316 mg sodium

Cranberry Meatballs

Serves 8
Active: 5 min
Total: 3 to 4 hr on low

1 can (16 oz) whole-berry or jellied cranberry sauce
¾ cup chili sauce
¼ cup water
2 bags (1 lb each) frozen fully cooked meatballs, completely thawed

❶ Put the cranberry sauce, chili sauce and water in slow cooker and stir to combine. Add the meatballs and stir to coat them with the sauce.
❷ Cover and cook on low 3 to 4 hours, until bubbly and meatballs are heated through.
❸ Stir and serve warm from the slow cooker.

Tip: Add 2 packed Tbsp brown sugar and 1 tsp lemon juice to the sauce for a sweet-sour variation.

Per serving: 441 calories, 22 g protein, 37 g carbohydrates, 8 g fiber, 25 g fat (12 g saturated fat), 40 mg cholesterol, 1,022 mg sodium

BBQ Beef Sandwich

Makes 8
Active: 5 min
Total: 8 to 10 hr on low, plus 15 min on high

1 medium onion, chopped
3½-lb bottom round beef roast, well trimmed of excess fat
¾ cup ketchup
½ cup cola
1 Tbsp each Dijon mustard and Worcestershire sauce
3 Tbsp cornstarch
¼ cup water
8 sandwich buns

❶ Place beef on onion in a 3½-qt or larger slow cooker. Mix ketchup, cola, mustard and Worcestershire sauce in a bowl; pour over beef.
❷ Cover and cook on low 8 to 10 hours. Remove beef to a plate; cover loosely with foil. Increase cooker heat to high. Stir cornstarch and water in a small cup until dissolved. Stir into liquid in cooker; cook 15 to 20 minutes until thickened.
❸ Thinly slice beef, layer on buns and spoon sauce over top.

Per sandwich: 462 calories, 48 g protein, 34 g carbohydrates, 1 g fiber, 13 g fat (4 g saturated fat), 117 mg cholesterol, 692 mg sodium

BBQ Ribs

Serves 6
Active: 5 min
Total: 6 to 8 hr on low

Great with cornbread and slaw.

2 medium onions
4 lb country-style pork ribs
1 cup Hot 'n Spicy barbecue sauce (we used KC Masterpiece; or your favorite sauce)

❶ Halve, then thinly slice onions. Place onions, then ribs and barbecue sauce in a 5-qt or larger slow cooker.
❷ Cover and cook on low 6 to 8 hours until ribs are tender.

Per serving: 549 calories, 36 g protein, 10 g carbohydrates, 1 g fiber, 39 g fat (13 g saturated fat), 142 mg cholesterol, 461 mg sodium

Different takes
- Add 1 lb rinsed fresh sauerkraut to cooker before adding ribs.
- Give ribs an Asian twist by adding minced garlic and ginger to teriyaki-flavor barbecue sauce.
- Stir canned baked beans into sauce in cooker 30 minutes before ribs will be done.

Cuban Ropa Vieja

Serves 4
Active: 15 min
Total: 8 to 10 hr on low

2 cubanelle or Italian frying peppers, seeded and sliced
1 cup sliced onion
1 can (8 oz) tomato sauce
¼ cup tomato paste
1 Tbsp each olive oil, cider vinegar and minced garlic
1 tsp ground cumin
1 bay leaf
½ tsp salt
1½-lb boneless chuck steak
⅓ cup coarsely chopped alcaparrado (we used Goya), or ⅓ cup pimiento-stuffed
     olives plus 2 Tbsp chopped capers
⅓ cup chopped cilantro

❶ Mix all ingredients except steak, alcaparrado and cilantro in a 3½-qt or larger slow cooker. Top with steak; turn steak over to coat with mixture.
❷ Cover and cook on low 8 to 10 hours until steak is very tender. Transfer steak to a cutting board. Remove and discard bay leaf. Tear steak into shreds using two forks. Return shreds to cooker; stir in alcaparrado and chopped cilantro and serve.

Per serving: 541 calories, 32 g protein, 15 g carbohydrates, 3 g fiber, 40 g fat (14 g saturated fat), 123 mg cholesterol, 1,098 mg sodium

Curried Lamb

Serves 6
Active: 10 min
Total: 8 to 10 hr on low

4 cups 1-in. chunks peeled butternut squash (about half of a 2½-lb squash)
1½ lb lamb stew meat
1 jar (15 oz) tikka masala cooking sauce
1 cup frozen peas

❶ Stir butternut squash, lamb and ¾ cup cooking sauce in a 3½-qt or larger slow cooker.
❷ Cover and cook on low 8 to 10 hours until lamb and butternut squash are tender.
Stir in peas and remaining cooking sauce 15 minutes before end of cooking.

Per serving: 398 calories, 23 g protein, 18 g carbohydrates, 3 g fiber, 26 g fat (10 g saturated fat), 79 mg cholesterol, 553 mg sodium

Greek Lamb & Spinach Stew

Serves 6
Active: 10 min
Total: 7 to 9 hr on low, plus 15 min on high

2-lb boneless lamb shoulder, visible fat trimmed, cut in 1-in. pieces
1 can (14.5 oz) diced tomatoes
½ cup chopped onion
1 Tbsp minced garlic
½ tsp each Greek herb seasoning and salt
¼ tsp pepper
1 can (19 oz) cannellini beans, rinsed
1 can (13.75 oz) whole artichoke hearts, cut in half
3 cups baby spinach (3 oz)
2 tsp grated lemon zest
Garnish: crumbled feta cheese

❶ Mix lamb pieces, tomatoes, onion, garlic, Greek seasoning, salt and pepper in a 3½-qt or larger slow cooker.

❷ Cover and cook on low 7 to 9 hours until lamb is tender when pierced.

❸ Mash 1 cup beans. Stir mashed and whole beans, artichoke hearts and spinach into cooker.

❹ Cover and cook on high 15 minutes or until spinach wilts and mixture is hot.

❺ Stir in lemon zest; sprinkle with feta. Serve with orzo.

Per serving: 325 calories, 36 g protein, 19 g carbohydrates, 6 g fiber, 11 g fat (4 g saturated fat), 100 mg cholesterol, 619 mg sodium

Sweet & Spicy Lamb Tagine

Serves 6
Active: 35 min
Total: 4 to 5 hr on high, or 8 to 10 hr on low

1 tsp each ground cumin, cinnamon, ginger and coriander
2 Tbsp olive oil
1 boneless leg of lamb (4 to 6 lb), trimmed of fat and cut into bite-size pieces
Salt and freshly ground black pepper, to taste
1½ cups chicken broth
2 large tomatoes, peeled, seeded and coarsely chopped
1 medium onion, chopped
1 leek, white part only, cleaned and sliced
2 medium carrots, peeled and chopped
1 pear, peeled and diced
½ cup raisins or sliced dates
Cooked couscous (optional)
¼ cup toasted pine nuts

❶ Combine cumin, cinnamon, ginger and coriander, and divide mixture in half.
❷ In a large nonstick skillet, heat 1 Tbsp of the oil over high heat; add lamb, half the spice mixture, and salt and pepper to taste. Brown the lamb well on all sides, then transfer it to a large slow cooker, draining any fat from the skillet.
❸ Heat remaining oil and spice mixture in the same skillet over medium heat until aromatic, about 20 to 30 seconds. Add to slow cooker. Add the chicken broth, tomatoes, onion, leek, carrots, pear and raisins; stir well.
❹ Cover and cook on high 4 to 5 hours, or on low 8 to 10 hours, until lamb is tender.
❺ To serve, spoon lamb mixture over couscous, if using, and sprinkle the pine nuts over all.

Per serving: 679 calories, 80 g protein, 25 g carbohydrates, 4 g fiber, 28 g fat (8 g saturated fat), 246 mg cholesterol, 765 mg sodium

Moo Shu Pork

Serves 10
Active: 10 min
Total: 6 to 9 hr on low

1 boneless pork loin roast (2 lb), fat trimmed, quartered lengthwise
1 cup hoisin sauce
1 Tbsp freshly grated ginger
6 cups shredded Napa cabbage
1½ cups shredded carrots
¼ cup sliced scallions
3 Tbsp rice wine vinegar
1½ Tbsp sugar
Flour tortillas, warmed

❶ Put pork, ⅓ cup hoisin sauce and ginger in a 3½-qt or larger slow cooker. Turn pork to coat.
❷ Cover and cook on low 6 to 9 hours until pork is very tender. Turn off cooker. Remove pork to a cutting board and, using two forks, pull meat into shreds.
❸ Toss cabbage, carrots, scallions, vinegar and sugar in a bowl to mix.
❹ Spread each tortilla with about 1½ tsp remaining hoisin sauce. Top with about ⅓ cup cabbage mixture and ¼ cup shredded pork.

Per serving: 418 calories, 27 g protein, 52 g carbohydrates, 5 g fiber, 11 g fat (3 g saturated fat), 54 mg cholesterol, 777 mg sodium

Sausage & Peppers Meat Loaf

Serves 8
Active: 10 min
Total: 5 to 8 hr on low

1½ cups Barilla Sweet Peppers & Garlic pasta sauce
1 lb hot or sweet Italian pork sausage, removed from casings
1 lb lean ground beef
¾ cup each fresh bread crumbs and finely chopped onion
¼ cup shredded Romano or Parmesan cheese
1 large egg
2 tsp minced garlic
2 tsp fennel seeds (optional)
½ tsp each salt and pepper

❶ To ease removal of loaf from cooker, fold two 24-in.-long pieces foil in half lengthwise twice. Place strips across each other, forming a "+" in bottom of a 3½-qt or larger slow cooker. Press strips against inside of cooker, letting ends hang over outside.
❷ Mix ½ cup pasta sauce with remaining ingredients in a large bowl until well blended. Form into a 7½ x 4½ x 2½-in. loaf. Place in cooker.
❸ Cover and cook on low 5 to 8 hours until a meat thermometer inserted in the center of the loaf registers 165°F.
❹ Heat rest of sauce; serve with meat loaf.

Tip: Try a pasta salad on the side. Leftover meat loaf makes great sandwiches.

Per serving: 410 calories, 21 g protein, 8 g carbohydrates, 1 g fiber, 32 g fat (12 g saturated fat), 115 mg cholesterol, 893 mg sodium

South Carolina BBQ Pork Sliders

Serves 8
Active: 15 min
Total: 8 to 10 hr on low

1 slow cooker liner
¼ cup packed brown sugar
2 Tbsp each paprika and dried minced onion
1½ tsp salt-free chili powder
1½ tsp salt
½ tsp garlic powder
½ tsp allspice (optional)
4 lb bone-in pork shoulder roast
¾ cup apple cider vinegar
½ cup sliced scallions
24 small dinner rolls, split
Accompaniments: hot pepper sauce, coleslaw

❶ Line a 4-qt or larger slow cooker with liner. Mix 1 Tbsp of the brown sugar, the paprika, minced onion, chili powder, salt, garlic powder and allspice. Sprinkle 1 Tbsp into bottom of slow cooker. Rub remaining mixture over pork. Add vinegar and remaining brown sugar to slow cooker; stir to mix. Add pork.
❷ Cover and cook on low 8 to 10 hours until pork is fork-tender. Remove pork to cutting board and pull into shreds. Return to slow cooker; add scallions and toss to coat.
❸ Put about ¼ cup onto each bun bottom. Top with bun tops.

Per serving (3 sliders): 596 calories, 39 g protein, 48 g carbohydrates, 3 g fiber, 26 g fat (9 g saturated fat), 110 mg cholesterol, 948 mg sodium

South Beach Mojo Pork

Serves 6
Active: 10 min
Total: 8 to 10 hr on low

1 cup Mojo Criollo Marinade (we used Goya)
1 jalapeño pepper, seeded and minced
1 clove garlic, minced
2½-lb boneless pork loin roast, well trimmed
2 navel oranges, peel and white pith removed, flesh cut into sections
½ cup thinly sliced red onion
¼ cup chopped cilantro

❶ Mix ¾ cup of the marinade, the pepper and garlic in a 3½-qt or larger slow cooker.
Add pork and turn to coat. (If you have time, cover and place in the refrigerator to let pork marinate for several hours, turning occasionally.)
❷ Cover and cook on low 8 to 10 hours until pork is tender.
❸ About 10 minutes before serving, combine oranges, onion and remaining ¼ cup marinade in a medium bowl. Leave at room temperature.
❹ Transfer pork to cutting board; slice. Skim fat from top of liquid in slow cooker.
Spoon liquid over sliced pork. Stir cilantro into orange mixture; top pork with mixture.

Per serving: 304 calories, 37 g protein, 9 g carbohydrates, 1 g fiber, 12 g fat (4 g saturated fat), 104 mg cholesterol, 810 mg sodium

Split Pea Soup

Serves 4
Active: 15 min
Total: 6 hr on high, or 12 hr on low

Serve with cornbread, or cut cornbread in cubes, toast in oven and serve as croutons.

1 lb dried green split peas
2 cups diced onions
1½ cups diced carrots
1 cup diced celery
2 tsp minced garlic
½ tsp pepper
3 chicken bouillon cubes
1¼ lb ham hock(s)

❶ Put all ingredients and 7 cups water in a 5½-qt or larger slow cooker.
❷ Cover and cook on high 6 hours or on low 12 hours until peas are very soft and fall apart.
❸ Remove ham. When cool enough to handle, cut meat off the bone, dice and return to soup.

Per serving: 551 calories, 40 g protein, 84 g carbohydrates, 10 g fiber, 8 g fat (2 g saturated fat), 32 mg cholesterol, 1,528 mg sodium

Ranchero Pork with Lime-Marinated Onions

Serves 8
Active: 18 min
Total: 8 to 10 hr on low

1 can (14 oz) Mild Red Enchilada Sauce (we used Old El Paso)
1 can (4 oz) diced green chiles
3½ lb bone-in pork shoulder roast, well trimmed
1 medium red onion, sliced
¼ cup fresh lime juice
½ cup chopped fresh cilantro
Serve with: warm corn tortillas

❶ Mix enchilada sauce and chiles in a 4-qt or larger slow cooker. Add pork; spoon sauce over top. Cover and cook on low 8 to 10 hours until pork is very tender.
❷ At least 20 minutes before serving, toss onion slices with lime juice in a medium bowl. Let stand, tossing once or twice until slightly wilted.
❸ Remove pork to a cutting board. Stir cilantro into mixture in slow cooker. Break pork into bite-size chunks with a wooden spoon and return to cooker; stir to combine.
❹ To serve: Spoon pork mixture on warmed tortillas, top with marinated onions, fold and eat.

Per serving: 268 calories, 29 g protein, 9 g carbohydrates, 1 g fiber, 12 g fat (4 g saturated fat), 97 mg cholesterol, 607 mg sodium

Spring Vegetable & Chicken Stew

Serves 6
Active: 15 min
Total: 5 to 8 hr on low, plus 10 to 15 min on high

1 slow cooker liner
1½ lb boneless, skinless chicken thighs, cut in chunks
2 cups baby carrots, halved lengthwise
1 large leek, white and light green parts only, sliced (2 cups)
1 Tbsp chopped fresh tarragon
1 jar (12 oz) chicken gravy
⅓ cup dry white wine
1 Tbsp flour
½ tsp salt
8 oz fresh asparagus, trimmed, cut in 1- to 2-in. lengths
⅓ cup thawed frozen peas

❶ Line a 3-qt or larger slow cooker with liner. Put chicken, carrots, leek and tarragon in slow cooker. Pour in gravy. Put wine, flour and salt in gravy jar; cover and shake to mix. Pour into slow cooker; toss to coat. Cover and cook on low 5 to 8 hours until chicken and vegetables are tender.
❷ Turn to high. Add asparagus; cover and cook on high 10 to 15 minutes until asparagus are crisp-tender. Stir in peas.

Per serving: 207 calories, 25 g protein, 15 g carbohydrates, 2 g fiber, 5 g fat (1 g saturated fat), 99 mg cholesterol, 567 mg sodium

Chicken Posole

Serves 4
Active: 10 min
Total: 3½ hr on high

1 can (15 oz) yellow or white hominy, drained
1 can (14.5 oz) Mexican-style diced tomatoes
1 can (10 oz) mild green enchilada sauce
2 carrots, diced
1 medium onion, chopped
3 garlic cloves, minced
2 tsp cumin
5 chicken thighs (1½ lb), skin removed
Chopped cilantro (optional)
Serve with: lime wedges, tortilla chips

❶ Combine hominy, tomatoes, enchilada sauce, carrots, onion, garlic and cumin in a 4-qt slow cooker. Add chicken and stir to combine. Cover and cook on high 3 to 3½ hours until chicken is cooked through and vegetables tender. Skim and discard any fat from the surface.
❷ Remove chicken; pull meat off bones into large shreds. Stir back into slow cooker. Stir in cilantro, if using. Serve with lime wedges and tortilla chips.

Per serving: 262 calories, 22 g protein, 26 g carbohydrates, 5 g fiber, 7 g fat (1 g saturated fat), 80 mg cholesterol, 1,083 mg sodium

Chicken & Vegetables with Creamy Mustard-Herb Sauce

Serves 4
Active: 15 min
Total: 7 to 9 hr on low

1 can (10.75 oz) condensed cream of chicken soup with herbs
2 leeks (about 8 oz), rinsed, white and light green parts thinly sliced (1½ cups),
   or 1½ cups sliced scallions
4 whole chicken thighs (about 2½ lb), skin removed
4 medium new potatoes (about 12 oz), cut in 1½-in. chunks
8 oz baby carrots (1¼ cups)
1 Tbsp Dijon mustard
2 Tbsp each snipped dill and sliced scallion

❶ Stir soup and leeks in a 3½-qt or larger slow cooker until blended. Add chicken, potatoes and carrots; stir to mix and coat.
❷ Cover and cook on low 7 to 9 hours until chicken, potatoes and carrots are tender when pierced.
❸ Remove chicken and vegetables to serving bowl with a slotted spoon. Add mustard to cooker; whisk until smooth. Stir in the dill and scallion; spoon over chicken and vegetables.

Per serving: 362 calories, 36 g protein, 31 g carbohydrates, 4 g fiber, 9 g fat (2 g saturated fat), 133 mg cholesterol, 769 mg sodium

Mango Chutney Chicken

Serves 4
Active: 10 min
Total: 6 to 8 hr on low, plus 15 min on high

8 chicken thighs (3¼ lb), skin removed
1 red bell pepper, quartered and sliced
1 jar (9 oz) mango chutney (¾ cup)
2 Tbsp lime juice (grate zest first)
2 tsp minced garlic
1½ tsp curry powder
¼ tsp each salt and freshly ground pepper
2 Tbsp cornstarch dissolved in 2 Tbsp water
1 firm-ripe mango, peeled and sliced
1 tsp grated lime zest
Serve with: couscous or rice, chopped peanuts

❶ Place chicken and peppers in a 3½-qt or larger slow cooker. Mix chutney, lime juice, garlic, curry powder, salt and pepper in medium bowl; pour over chicken.
❷ Cover and cook on low 6 to 8 hours until chicken is cooked through.
❸ Remove chicken and peppers to serving platter; stir in cornstarch mixture and mango. Increase heat to high; cook, covered, 15 minutes or until slightly thickened. Stir in lime zest. Spoon sauce over chicken; serve with couscous or rice and chopped peanuts.

Per serving: 463 calories, 42 g protein, 53 g carbohydrates, 2 g fiber, 9 g fat (2 g saturated fat), 174 mg cholesterol, 1,147 mg sodium

Chicken with Kielbasa & Rice

Serves 6
Active: 15 min
Total: 7 to 8 hr on low

2 cups each sliced onion and celery
4 cloves garlic, crushed
1¼ cups chicken broth
6 chicken drumsticks (1¾ lb), skin removed
1 tsp paprika
½ tsp salt
¼ tsp pepper
1 lb kielbasa, sliced
2 cups 5-minute rice
1 large red pepper, cut in narrow strips
Garnish: chopped scallions

❶ Mix onion, celery, garlic and broth in a 5½-qt or larger slow cooker.
❷ Rub drumsticks with paprika, salt and pepper. Add to cooker along with the kielbasa.
❸ Cover and cook on low 7 to 8 hours until chicken is tender. Remove drumsticks to a large plate and cover to keep warm.
❹ Add rice and pepper strips to cooker. Cover and cook 15 minutes, or until rice and pepper are tender. Sprinkle servings with scallions.

Per serving: 479 calories, 29 g protein, 36 g carbohydrates, 2 g fiber, 23 g fat (8 g saturated fat), 106 mg cholesterol, 1,228 mg sodium

Chicken with Potatoes & Olives

Serves 6
Active: 10 min
Total: 5 hr on high, or 8 hr on low

3 large all-purpose potatoes, peeled and cut bite-size
1 large green pepper, cut in narrow strips
1 medium onion, chopped
1 can (15 oz) tomato sauce
½ cup dry white wine
½ cup pimiento-stuffed olives
1½ Tbsp each minced garlic and olive oil
1 Tbsp tomato paste
½ tsp each salt and pepper
1 bay leaf, broken in half
6 each chicken drumsticks and thighs (about 3 lb), skin and excess fat removed

❶ Put all ingredients except chicken in a 4½-qt or larger cooker; stir to mix. Add chicken; stir to coat.
❷ Cover and cook on high 5 hours or on low 8 hours, or until chicken is cooked through and tender and potatoes can be easily pierced. Discard bay leaf.

Per serving: 340 calories, 35 g protein, 26 g carbohydrates, 4 g fiber, 11 g fat (2 g saturated fat), 123 mg cholesterol, 1,056 mg sodium

Apple Chicken Curry

Serves 8
Active: 15 min
Total: 4 hr on low

2½ lb boneless, skinless chicken thighs and/or breasts
¾ tsp salt
½ tsp freshly ground black pepper
2 apples, peeled if desired, cored and cut in ½-in.-thick slices
3 cups green and/or red bell pepper, seeded and cut in chunks
1 can (about 14 oz) diced tomatoes, undrained
1 cup apple juice
1 Tbsp curry powder
2 tsp chopped garlic
½ cup raisins
Cooked rice (optional)

❶ Sprinkle chicken pieces with salt and pepper; place in a 3½-qt or larger slow cooker along with apples.
❷ In a large skillet, combine bell peppers, tomatoes with their juices, apple juice, curry powder and garlic; bring to a boil. Stir in raisins. Pour over chicken and apples in slow cooker.
❸ Cover and cook on low 4 hours, or until chicken is cooked through. Serve over cooked rice, if desired.

Per serving: 251 calories, 32 g protein, 22 g carbohydrates, 3 g fiber, 4 g fat (1 g saturated fat), 100 mg cholesterol, 524 mg sodium

Chicken Paprikash

Serves 4
Active: 10 min
Total: 8 to 10 hr on low

4 each chicken drumsticks and thighs (about 2½ lb), skin removed
1 can (10.75 oz) 25%-less-sodium cream of mushroom soup
2 Tbsp paprika
½ cup nonfat sour cream

1 Place chicken in 3½-qt or larger slow cooker. Stir soup and paprika in small bowl until blended. Spoon soup mixture over chicken to cover.

2 Cover and cook on low 8 to 10 hours until chicken is tender. Remove chicken with slotted spoon to serving platter. Whisk sour cream into the cooking liquid. Serve sauce over chicken.

Per serving: 297 calories, 35 g protein, 12 g carbohydrates, 2 g fiber, 12 g fat (2 g saturated fat), 135 mg cholesterol, 598 mg sodium

Jamaican Jerk BBQ Chicken

Serves 4
Active: 5 min
Total: 6 to 8 hr on low

Great with coleslaw and cornbread on the side.

8 chicken drumsticks (about 2 lb), skin removed
2 tsp Caribbean jerk seasoning
¾ cup barbecue sauce
1 Tbsp dark rum (optional)
¼ cup sliced scallions

❶ Rub drumsticks with seasoning. Place in a 3½-qt or larger slow cooker. Pour barbecue sauce and rum over chicken. Turn chicken to coat.

❷ Cover and cook on low 6 to 8 hours until chicken is tender. Sprinkle with scallions.

Per serving: 188 calories, 27 g protein, 6 g carbohydrates, 1 g fiber, 5 g fat (1 g saturated fat), 98 mg cholesterol, 635 mg sodium

Thai Chicken Legs with Vegetables

Serves 4
Active: 15 min
Total: 6 to 8 hr on low

1 can (14 oz) lite or regular coconut milk (not cream of coconut)
¼ cup flour
1 Tbsp each Thai red curry base (such as A Taste of Thai) and minced garlic
1 tsp salt
4 each chicken drumsticks and thighs (about 2½ lb), skin and excess fat removed
1 medium onion, halved and thinly sliced
2 large carrots, thinly sliced
1 medium bell pepper, quartered and sliced
2 cups frozen cut okra or green beans
Garnish: fresh mint leaves, cut in strips

❶ Whisk coconut milk, flour and curry base in a 4-qt or larger slow cooker until smooth. Whisk in garlic and salt. Add chicken, onion and carrots; stir to mix. Scatter bell pepper over top.

❷ Cover and cook on low 6 to 8 hours until chicken and vegetables are tender. Stir in frozen okra; cover and cook 5 minutes or until crisp-tender. Remove chicken and vegetables to serving bowl with a slotted spoon. Whisk sauce in cooker until smooth. Pour over chicken and vegetables. Sprinkle servings with mint.

Per serving: 408 calories, 44 g protein, 28 g carbohydrates, 7 g fiber, 14 g fat (5 g saturated fat), 154 mg cholesterol, 944 mg sodium

Turkey-Corn Soup

Serves: 4
Active: 5 min
Total: 8 to 10 hr on low

2 turkey thighs (1 lb each), skin removed
1 medium onion, chopped
1 can (15.5 oz) white kidney beans (cannellini), rinsed
1 can (11 oz) corn, drained
1½ cups medium-hot tomatillo salsa
1 can (4.5 oz) chopped green chiles
2 tsp minced garlic
1½ tsp ground cumin
½ tsp salt
⅓ cup chopped cilantro
Serve with: sour cream, Monterey Jack cheese

❶ Put turkey thighs and onion in a 3½-qt or larger slow cooker. Add beans and corn. Mix salsa, chiles, garlic, cumin and salt in a medium bowl; pour over all.
❷ Cover and cook on low 8 to 10 hours until meat is tender. Remove turkey to a cutting board and cut into bite-size pieces.
❸ Return meat to cooker; stir in cilantro.

Per serving: 427 calories, 44 g protein, 37 g carbohydrates, 8 g fiber, 10 g fat (3 g saturated fat), 115 mg cholesterol, 1,087 mg sodium

Tip: If you can get it, try grating some Dry Jack cheese over the soup. It's Monterey Jack that's been aged, so it packs a punchier taste.

Vegetable Curry

Serves 6
Active: 5 min
Total: 6 to 7 hr on low

1 can (14 oz) light coconut milk
¼ cup flour
1½ Tbsp red curry paste
1 large onion, chopped
4 small Yukon gold potatoes, halved
4 cups butternut squash, cut in 1½-in. chunks
4 cups cauliflower florets
1 can (15 oz) chickpeas, rinsed
1 red bell pepper, cut in 1-in. pieces
1 cup frozen peas
3 cups cooked basmati rice
Garnish: chopped cilantro

❶ Whisk coconut milk, flour and curry paste in a 3½-qt or larger slow cooker. Stir in all vegetables except peas; mix well.
❷ Cover and cook on low 6 to 7 hours until vegetables are tender. Stir in peas, cover and let sit 5 minutes. Serve with rice; garnish with cilantro.

Per serving: 355 calories, 11 g protein, 63 g carbohydrates, 10 g fiber, 7 g fat (3 g saturated fat), 0 mg cholesterol, 244 mg sodium

Vegetarian Chili

Serves 6 (makes 7 cups)
Active: 15 min
Total: 6 to 8 hr on low

1 slow cooker liner
1 small sweet onion, finely chopped
2 medium poblano peppers, chopped
1 Tbsp minced garlic (3 cloves)
1 can (15 oz) red kidney beans, rinsed
1 can (15 oz) black beans, rinsed
1 can (15 oz) chickpeas, rinsed
1 cup frozen corn niblets
1 jar (16 oz) smooth chipotle or roja salsa
1 can (8 oz) tomato sauce
¾ cup water
2 Tbsp cocoa chili spice blend or unsweetened cocoa
2 Tbsp salt-free chili powder
2 tsp ground cumin
⅓ cup chopped cilantro
Serve with: sour cream, shredded cheese, toasted pumpkin seeds

❶ Line a 3-qt or larger slow cooker with liner. Mix all ingredients except cilantro in slow cooker. Cover and cook on low 6 to 8 hours until vegetables are tender and flavors are blended.
❷ Stir in cilantro. Top with sour cream, cheese and/or toasted pumpkin seeds.

Per serving: 323 calories, 16 g protein, 62 g carbohydrates, 18 g fiber, 3 g fat (0 g saturated fat), 0 mg cholesterol, 942 mg sodium

Italian Lentil & Vegetable Stew

Serves 5
Active: 5 min
Total: 8 to 10 hr on low

1½ cups dried lentils
3 cups butternut squash, cut in 1-in. chunks
2 cups bottled marinara sauce
2 cups green beans, ends trimmed and beans cut in half
1 red bell pepper, cut in 1-in. pieces
1 large all-purpose potato, peeled and cut in 1-in. chunks
¾ cup chopped onion
1 tsp minced garlic
1 Tbsp olive oil, preferably extra-virgin
Serve with: grated Parmesan

❶ Mix lentils and 3 cups water in a 3-qt or larger slow cooker. In a large bowl, mix remaining ingredients except olive oil; place over lentils.
❷ Cover and cook on low 8 to 10 hours until vegetables and lentils are tender. Stir in the oil. Serve in soup plates or bowls. Serve Parmesan in a bowl separately.

Per serving: 383 calories, 21 g protein, 66 g carbohydrates, 12 g fiber, 7 g fat (1 g saturated fat), 0 mg cholesterol, 644 mg sodium

Pasta with Ratatouille

Serves 6
Active: 7 min
Total: 5 to 8 hr on low

1 medium onion, chopped
3 garlic cloves, chopped
1 medium eggplant
3 medium zucchini
2 green bell peppers
6 plum tomatoes
1 can (8 oz) tomato sauce
1 Tbsp each chopped fresh oregano and thyme (or 1 tsp each dried)
½ tsp each salt and pepper
2 Tbsp each red wine vinegar and extra-virgin olive oil
1 lb rigatoni pasta
Serve with: grated Parmesan

❶ Place onion and garlic in a 6-qt slow cooker.
❷ Cut eggplant, zucchini, peppers and tomatoes into 1-in. chunks; toss in large bowl with tomato sauce, herbs, salt and pepper. Add to slow cooker.
❸ Cook on low 5 to 8 hours until vegetables are tender. Stir in vinegar and oil.
❹ Bring a large pot of lightly salted water to a boil. Add pasta and cook as package directs; toss with ratatouille. Serve with Parmesan.

Per serving: 360 calories, 12 g protein, 69 g carbohydrates, 7 g fiber, 4 g fat (1 g saturated fat), 0 mg cholesterol, 256 mg sodium

Cioppino

Serves 6
Active: 10 min
Total: 7 to 9 hr on low, plus 20 to 40 min on high

2 cups thinly sliced fennel
2 leeks (white and pale green parts only), rinsed and thinly sliced (1 cup)
12 oz small red potatoes, quartered
1 jar (26 oz) marinara sauce
1 can (14.5 oz) chicken broth
1 cup water
⅓ cup dry red wine (optional)
1 tsp fennel seeds (optional)
¼ tsp hot pepper flakes
24 cleaned mussels
12 sea scallops, halved if very large
1 lb skinless halibut fillet, cut into 1½-in. chunks
Serve with: sourdough bread and olive oil for drizzling

❶ Mix all ingredients except seafood in a 5-qt or larger slow cooker.
❷ Cover and cook on low 7 to 9 hours until vegetables are tender.
❸ Raise heat to high; stir in seafood. Cover and cook 20 to 40 minutes until mussels open and seafood is cooked.

Per serving: 297 calories, 33 g protein, 28 g carbohydrates, 4 g fiber, 6 g fat (1 g saturated fat), 54 mg cholesterol, 943 mg sodium

Portuguese Shrimp & Sausage Soup

Serves 4
Active: 10 min
Total: 6 to 9 hr on low, plus 15 min on high

1 can (14.5 oz) fire-roasted diced tomatoes
4 red potatoes (8 oz), quartered
8 oz chorizo sausage, sliced ½ in. thick
1 large cubanelle or Italian frying pepper, quartered and sliced (1 cup)
1 stalk celery, thinly sliced (½ cup)
½ cup each white wine and water
¼ cup finely chopped onion
½ tsp smoked paprika (optional)
½ tsp minced garlic
¼ tsp each salt and dried thyme
1 lb (31 to 40) medium shrimp, peeled and deveined, thawed if frozen
Garnish: cilantro (optional)

❶ Place all ingredients except shrimp in a 3-qt or larger slow cooker. Gently stir until well combined and vegetables are covered in cooking liquid. Cover and cook on low 6 to 9 hours until vegetables are tender.
❷ Turn heat to high. Add shrimp to slow cooker, pushing them down into soup. Cover and cook on high 15 minutes or until shrimp are just cooked through. Garnish with cilantro, if desired.

Per serving: 446 calories, 35 g protein, 21 g carbohydrates, 2 g fiber, 23 g fat (8 g saturated fat), 190 mg cholesterol, 1,228 mg sodium

New England Seafood Chowder

Serves 6
Active: 15 min
Total: 6 to 8 hr on low

2 leeks, halved lengthwise and thinly sliced (white and light green parts only)
8 oz red new potatoes, cut in eighths
1½ cups fresh corn or 1 can (11 oz) corn niblets, drained
1 can (10 oz) condensed cream of celery soup
1½ cups water
1 bay leaf
¼ tsp dried thyme
⅛ tsp ground red pepper (cayenne)
8 oz cod fillets, cut into 1-in. chunks
8 oz raw large shrimp, peeled
1 cup milk
4 slices precooked bacon (from a 2.1-oz box)

❶ Place leeks, potatoes and corn in a 3½-qt or larger slow cooker. Add soup, water, bay leaf, thyme and cayenne; mix gently.
❷ Cover and cook on low 6 to 8 hours until potatoes are tender. Add seafood about 15 minutes before serving; heat until fish is just cooked through. Stir in milk; remove bay leaf. Remove from heat.
❸ Heat bacon as package directs; crumble over bowls of chowder.

Per serving: 250 calories, 20 g protein, 28 g carbohydrates, 3 g fiber, 7 g fat (2 g saturated fat), 88 mg cholesterol, 628 mg sodium

Jambalaya

Serves 5
Active: 10 min
Total: 4½ to 5½ hr on low

1 medium red onion, finely chopped
1 green bell pepper, chopped
2 ribs celery, thinly sliced
8 oz turkey kielbasa, sliced
1 can (28 oz) whole tomatoes
1 cup uncooked converted rice
2 tsp salt-free Cajun-Creole seasoning (we used The Spice Hunter)
12 oz peeled large shrimp (21 to 25 count)
Garnish: chopped parsley and hot pepper sauce

❶ Layer onion, pepper, celery and turkey kielbasa in a 3½-qt or larger slow cooker.
❷ Mix tomatoes and their juices, rice and seasoning in medium bowl, breaking up tomatoes with a spoon. Pour into slow cooker. Cover and cook on low 4 to 5 hours until vegetables and rice are tender.
❸ Stir in shrimp, cover and cook 20 minutes or until cooked through. Sprinkle with parsley and hot sauce.

Per serving: 325 calories, 26 g protein, 44 g carbohydrates, 3 g fiber, 5 g fat (1 g saturated fat), 133 mg cholesterol, 744 mg sodium

Photo Credits